POEMS OF LOVE & RELATIONSHIPS

BECAUSE SHE DECIDED TO LOVE

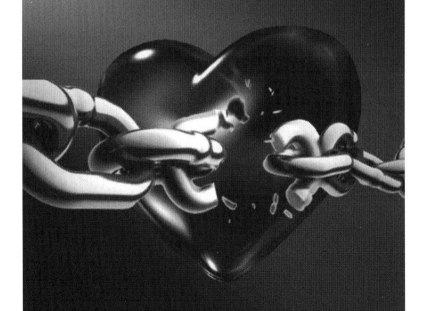

KATRINA A. MCCAIN

KATRINA A. MCCAIN

shero
publishing

PO Box, Raleigh, NC 27616
SHEROPublishing.com
Contact the Publisher: ericaperrygreen@gmail.com
For copies and publishing information, contact: SHEROPublishing.com

Cover & Design Layout: Greenlight Creations - glightcreations.com
Editing: Synergyed Consulting

Printed by: Impress Print & Graphics
P.O. Box 13794 RTP, NC 27709

Printed in the United States of America
Library of Congress Cataloging-in-Publication Data
ISBN: 978-0-9998789-6-5

BECAUSE SHE DECIDED TO LOVE

KATRINA A. MCCAIN

A COLLECTION OF POEMS

TABLE OF CONTENTS

Dedication

This book is dedicated to the best parts of me….

Arrius Lavey McCain
&
Angela LeAnn McCain

LOVE IS PATIENT,
LOVE IS KIND.
IT DOES NOT ENVY,
IT DOES NOT BOAST,
IT IS NOT PROUD.
IT DOES NOT DISHONOR OTHERS,
IT IS NOT SELF-SEEKING,
IT IS NOT EASILY ANGERED,
IT KEEPS NO RECORD OF WRONGS.

1 Corinthians 13:4-5

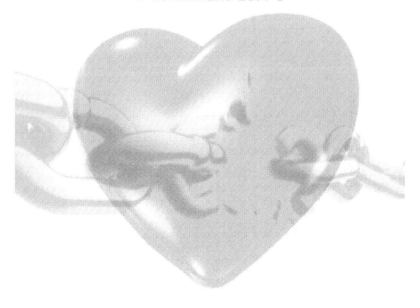

Acknowledgements

WOW.... this really happened! None of this would have been possible if I had not been obedient one night at the beach with my family. Numerous ideas floated in my head regarding the first poem I wrote after a 20 year break from writing. I wanted to do nothing but sleep after chasing the sun all day. As I began to write ideas down, the poem took a life of its own and transformed into something uniquely beautiful.

First, I humbly thank God Almighty for giving me a creative way to express every day thoughts and experiences. Despite my shortcomings, God's love runs deeper and deeper for me; so much so, he protected this unused gift of poetry. He tugged on me so long that I had no choice but to pick up a pen again. I will guard this gift with my life as a reflection of my gratitude and appreciation.

To my amazing Son and my more amazing Granddaughter... words can't express the love I have for you or the joy you bring to my life. EVERYTHING I do is done out of love for you. I live the life I live because I want you two to look at me one day and be proud of me, like I am of you. My eyes beam when I talk about you two, and my heart leaps when I think of you loving me back. The sky is the limit to the amazing things God has in store for you. Always remember your upbringings by staying humble, stay close to God's unchanging hand and ALWAYS forgive people and yourself in ALL situations.

To my McCain and Richardson families, my ride or dies who feel like family and to my friends still by my side after years of knowing each other... thank you for believing in me and supporting my vision. Many of you endured ideas of unfinished poems and never seemed annoyed. Thanks Momma for the sacrifices you made for your Girls and Grandchildren. We appreciate you from the bottom of our hearts. To my Daddy and

Stepdad.... you were two strong pillars in my life whose presence is missed daily. The things you taught me Daddy, still shape the woman I am today. I see you so much in the mirror and I hope I make you proud by honoring the values and principles you instilled in me. Finally, to my sisters.... tears are welling in my eyes as I try to describe what your support means to me. Through the ups and downs and through the thick and thin, I ALWAYS knew you had my back. Thank you Babes! You guys gave me more people to love; my beautiful nieces and nephews hold a huge part of my heart as well. Nieces and nephews, continue to leave your footprints all over this world. They will never be ready for your full potential once it bursts forward.

Finally, to myself... smile because this is you fulfilling a dream placed in your heart. You are beautiful inside and out and I'm more proud of you than words can say. On tough days, think about the goodness of Jesus and all he has done for you instead of that thing in front of your face. You got this Babe! Forever my number one girl!

Meet the Author

Author & Poet Katrina A. McCain

P oet Katrina A. McCain grew up in a small town named Nashville, NC and now resides in Greensboro, NC. She graduated from Guilford College in Greensboro, NC with a BS in Accounting. She currently works as an Accountant at a non-profit agency serving the youth in Guilford County, NC. Each year, she raises money for The America Cancer Society to support her battle with cancer and others fighting as well. She is a dedicated member of her family and always puts others first. Katrina stopped writing poetry when she was in her early 20s and dove back into her passion a couple of years ago. She wrote under the beloved name Kandi, producing countless unpublished pieces. *Because She Decided To Love* is her debut poetry book where her journey of love has taken her many interesting places. She passionately describes scenarios so vividly that raw emotions are felt in every poem. With the completion of this book, Katrina has already planned her next project.

Follow Poet Katrina A. McCain

Facebook: www.facebook.com/poetkatrinamccain
Instagram: @poetkatrinamccain

Introduction

I wrote my first poetry book about *love*, because I am its biggest fan, and honestly, I have been doing it wrongly 50% of the time. Wildly chasing after *love* for years, I still do not know the magic formula for its success. However, I have tons of feelings, on the subject, that I wanted to share with the world.

I was twelve years old the first time I wrote a poem. It was an assignment for my English class. I remember the excitement of forming the perfect words together to impress my teacher, who was usually unimpressed. At age 18, I became a mother and my son became the center of my world. All of my dreams and plans for my life were put on hold to ensure that he had the best upbringing I could offer him. While I loved poetry, life happened and I took a 20-year break from writing.

Because She Decided to Love started to take form when the poem, "That Space" was copyrighted. I had no intentions of writing a poetry book until I started receiving good reviews from the poem. Shockingly enough, a publishing company reached out to me to publish an entire book. With only two or three incomplete poems at the time, I made a decision that day…. I was going to explore the idea of writing an entire poetry book and sharing my collection of poems with the world.

For two years, I wrote poems, and the common theme seemed to be *love*. As hard as I tried to veer away from the topic; *love* showed up in every poem, whether it was a romantic *love*, *love* for my family and friends, the effects of *love* and most importantly… God's *love*. Once most of the poems were complete, I prayed about a title that would sum up all of the poems collectively. *Because She Decided to Love* was given to me in my prayer time. God never fails.

Please take this roller-coaster ride of raw emotions with me. All of the poems are loosely based off different personal experiences with *love* and the aftermath of those experiences. As I reread the poems over and over again, it was as if I was being introduced to the emotions involved in each of them for the first time. After reading this poetry book, you will be encouraged, even after heartbreak; *love* is the most beautiful thing in this world. There is no way we can live without *love*!

Poet Katrina A. McCain

LOVING ME– PERSONAL POEMS

Old Photo

T ime goes by before I think about you
Tucked safely away in my wallet.
Lying in a secure place behind who I am
You secretly know your importance in my life.
Mounds of plastic reveal my true identity
While I value your faded grayness like a gem.
Numbers tell where I live and how to reach me
Receipts show trends of my favorite purchases.
None of them can measure the uniqueness of you
Your blackness fades slowly to whiteness over time.
Your torn, fragile edges protectively hold his smile
Sadly, the world will never acknowledge your beauty.
As your age shows signs of an outdated method
Your value discombobulates the world's currency system.
Dirty, old money bangs its chest to establish dominancy
Your bumpy, texture attracts unimportant critics.
You quietly lie in the deepest, darkest part of my wallet
Tenderly preserving the first man I ever loved.
As I hold you lovely in my fingertips, I begin to reminisce
The memory you hold so dearly was once in my life.
Memory and I grew together and always put each other first
Tears flow from my eyes as I count the years gone by.
Magically, you release his famous words for me
"Who loves you Baby" in Daddy's voice.
Black and white have never been so colorful!

Before Momma Came Home

I should have known
Trouble was in the distance
When the sky rumbled.
I one-upped by sisters
With the best prank ever last week
Before Momma Came Home.
I stood by the window
Oblivious to the games
My sisters began to play.
The rain started softly
Dampening the pavement
Causing small puddles.
My smile grew bigger
As the lightening danced
Above our house.
Loud cracks of thunder
Roared through the heavens
Causing me to become antsier.
Anticipating the end of the storm
I leaped with joy
The pot of gold was mine!
The sun started to shine
As the rainbow settled
Across the beautiful sky.
Encouraged by sisters to hurry
I swiftly ran across the field
With thoughts of my pot of gold.
A few raindrops
Brushed against my skin
As I got closer and closer.

I slide directly under the rainbow
One shoe on my foot
The other shoe dangling alongside.
Shaking off the confusion
As laughter grew louder
From amongst my sisters.
They laced my shoes together
Raced passed me to steal my pot of gold
Before Momma came home.

Who Am I

W ho I am can be described in 5 simple words
An. Emotional. Walking. Time. Bomb.
I tap into every single emotion every day.
Every. Single. Emotion. Every. Single. Day.
Disgust is the first emotion of the day
Because my alarm clock screams at least three times before I move
How rude is it to be woken up like that every morning?
Disgust doesn't play about our sleep.
As soon as disgust calms down, anger shows its ugly face.
I needed to be at work five minutes before I set the house alarm.
Anger shakes his head at my aggressive driving.
I often turn into the parking lot at work on two wheels.
He should have buckled his seat beat tighter.
Surprise greets me in the hallway as I tiptoe in the building.
He honestly can't believe my arrival time AGAIN
Especially after I told him I was going to do better.
Surprise gets tired of fighting with me every day
Never taking into consideration I'm tired of fighting too.
Now fear is a tricky little guy trying to establish an unwanted place.
Every time I thumb him under my desk
He returns even louder and nagging me even more.
I squish him with my new shoe and sadness shows up.
I didn't have to do fear like that is sadness' point or view.
Fear's funeral will be held next week in the nearest bathroom.
The nerve of sadness to have empathy for fear's short lived life.
Little does sadness know, happiness is here to dismiss him.
I am biased towards happiness because she is my girl.
We work together, dance together and drink coffee together.
Happiness laughs at ALL my jokes
Even the ones others don't see as humorous.
Gracefully staying with me all day and brightening my nights
Finally, I escort this queen to bed with a smile.

I am so proud of happiness for her day's work.
I wasn't kidding when I said at the end of every single day
Who I am can be described in 5 simple words
An. Emotional. Walking. Time. Bomb.

My Blemished Past

Fueled by self-gratification
My Blemished Past resurfaces
No longer able to find the Old Me
Stumped by the newness
Redemption is sought elsewhere
The new Old Me confuses my Blemished Past

Harmless Lies?

The only time I thought it was right to lie was...
I told my son that Santa Claus was real.
I looked into those beautiful brown eyes
And created the BEST childhood he could ever asked.
Getting stuck in the crawl space or sliding in mud in my PJs
Neither mattered as long as I pulled off the perfect Christmas lie.

Because the Santa Claus lie was going so good...
I decided to lie about the Tooth Fairy too.
Those beautiful brown eyes tricked me again
And I found yet another way to make the best childhood BETTER.
I would sneak into his room like a ninja with two dollars in hand
Hide the money and sneak out like Spiderman... I was never there.

Acknowledging the fact that I was killing parenthood...
My next lie was the Easter Bunny.
Because my son was too smart for his own good
He questioned the logic behind the Bunny bringing Easter Eggs.
He asked if he could see Santa Claus and the Tooth Fairy the next time.
My late night character changing activities were in jeopardy.

One tragic night, when I was sleeping really hard
I forgot I was supposed to become the Tooth Fairy.
I snuck into his room at day break to slide two dollars under the pillow.
My son caught my hand and screamed aaaah.
Cold busted like a deer caught in headlights.
I did the only thing I could think after all the lies...
Lie even more and his childhood was never the same.

Pancakes In The Morning

T he sweetest smell tickled my nose
As the sun warmed my face.
Knowing what NaNa was up to in the kitchen
I ran to the bathroom like a deer.
Taking a million hours to brush my teeth
I jumped around like a frog.
Thousands of germs were next
As I scrubbed my hands with soap.
The hallway seemed a mile long
As music bounced around the house.
Entering the kitchen was magical
Like walking into a princess' castle.
My favorite cup and plate were on the table
Sprinkled with the brightest yellow.
I leaped into my NaNa's arms
As a smile as big as the ocean greeted me.
Mountains of pancakes were waiting for me
As the syrup danced beside my plate.
Blessing my food was the only thing
Stopping me from attacking those pancakes.
As I pounced on my plate of food
My heart was beating out of my chest.
When I finally came up for air
NaNa and I had another warm talk
That soothes my soul and makes me happy.
Candy and chocolate milk are so good
But there is nothing like Pancakes in the Morning.

Cancer Never Takes
A Vacation

Your bags are packed and ready to go at a moment's notice.
You are not interested in flying to a remote island.
You never reward yourself by having a drink on the beach.
You don't seem to be interested in relaxing by the poolside.
A Night Out on the town with your friends isn't desired.
Cancer never takes a vacation!

Instead you unpack your heavy luggage in my life.
You greet me every morning as the sun greets the day.
Escaping you is momentary as you seem to know where
I am at all times.
You follow me throughout my days by penetrating my thoughts.
You swing harder at me as I stand on "by Jesus Stripes I am healed".
New days become new challenges for you to destroy.
Cancer never takes a vacation!

Unwillingly traveling from one amazing place to another
You become the spectator in the museum of lost artifacts.
You have a front row seat to accomplishments your presence
couldn't hinder.
You wonder how the vacation you refused to take relaxed
your intentions.
You tremble as laughter resounds from pure happiness within me.
Cancer never takes a vacation!

KATRINA A. McCAIN

SEEKING LOVE-
DATING

Bleep, Bleep

My relaxation was really deep.
It was a quarter after neap.
I couldn't stop dreaming of this creep.
It started on a date that was cheap.
He was handsome, very zeap.
He had a reputation to upkeep.
My dislike for him started to seep.
I ran him over with my Jeep.
My horn was stuck on beep, beep.
The damaged bumper was in a heap.
The metal was a pile of scrapheap.
Sirens sounded to help him keep.
His safety was confirmed by a peep.
I only knocked him asleep.
My involvement couldn't be so deep.
The price to pay would be steep.
Crap I had to run away... bleep, bleep.
The fence I crossed with a huge leap.
A ran through a field with lots of sheep.
I disturbed them as they were sleep.
Why were they in a slapheap?
Exhausted so I started to weep.
I've sown now I accepted I must reap.
My alarm wakes me so I wouldn't oversleep.

Anything Doesn't Go
With a Scorpio

E ssentially, anything doesn't go with a Scorpio.
Capricorn was disciplined and all about his business
        While he experienced much success, he expected the worst.
An original, authentic love from Aquarius rocked my world
However, he was too temperamental and too stubborn for me.
Pisces loved me more compassionately than the rest
Until he played victim to his own created circumstances.
Honesty was a desired quality as trusting Aries was easy
Sadly, he was too impatient to learn me and build with me.
Stability offered by Taurus was desired and welcomed
Nevertheless, he was uncompromising when disagreements occurred
Gemini's flattery words of affection played on my passion
But his inconsistences revealed two personalities and broken promises
Cancer persuaded me to go after my dreams and set goals
Conversely, he became jealous of my celebrated achievements.
Generosity and creativity moved, governed and ruled Leo's life
Yet, he didn't leave enough room for me in his self-centered world.
Virgo's hard work, determination and go-get-it drive were attractive
Nonetheless, he was overly critical of our slow, steady progress.
Libra was fair minded and his cooperation was greatly appreciated
Unfortunately, he held grudges from past misunderstandings.
The hottest and unforgettable experiences were with Scorpio
Regrettably, our natural instincts kicked in and we couldn't trust each
other.
Giggling at Sagittarius' endless jokes was dope and light hearted
Still, he purposely engaged in tactless arguments for validation.
Conclusively, anything doesn't go with a Scorpio.

One Dance

A mbience was exotic and stimulating.
Lights were alluring and enticing.
People were attractive and sexy.
Music was relaxing and erotic.

Blushing, giggling and hiding my face.
Smiling, staring and biting your lip.
Surrendering to the magnetic attraction.
Awaiting in open space was One Dance.

Temptation ruled our sensibility.
Passion dominated our minds and bodies.
Seduction controlled the dance floor.
Fascination caused our One Dance.

My eyes danced with your eyes.
My voice danced with your voice.
My body danced with your body.
My mind danced with your mind.

One Dance changed strangers.
One Dance introduced soul mates.
One Dance brought new matrimony.
One Dance bonded two worlds.

Butterflies and a Perfect Stranger in Dark Lights

I ntrigued by a Perfect Stranger in Dark Lights
   I missed the Butterflies developing in my stomach.
If only for one night, I absolutely lost myself
To the sway of his words along with my hips.
My body fit perfectly against his body
Like the missing puzzle piece to his life.
His hands gently explored my body
Perfectly enough for strangers not to be offended.
Butterflies ran wildly through my mind
As curiosity planted its seed in Dark Lights.
Excitement and nervousness battled for victory
As a Perfect Stranger began whispering in my ear
You gonna be my girlfriend and this is your last first dance.
I now felt like the most beautiful woman in the room.
Butterflies once again took over in Dark Lights.
Calming my nerves as we exit the crowd to talk
I noticed his attractive personality and his sense of humor.
Our laughter sliced the Dark Lights and Butterflies like a sword.
His conversation held me in a trance.
I began to thirst for more of a Perfect Stranger.
How can I fairly judge a Perfect Stranger in Dark Lights?
My intuition said nothing or gave me a reasonable clue about the Butterflies.
I boldly stepped outside my comfort zone and asked for his phone number.
As numbers rolled smoothly off his tongue
I completely forgot about the Butterflies in Dark Lights.
Mesmerized by a Perfect Stranger's forwardness
Blinded by those hypnotic and Dark Lights
Choked by those beautiful Butterflies
I accepted the challenge proposed by a Perfect Stranger.
No games, no drama or past mistakes... a Perfect Stranger and me.

With all those Butterflies confusing my senses
I allowed a Perfect Stranger to lead me away from the
Dark Lights.

What's My Name?

I bragged he will never forget my name on every date we had.
He might be lucky enough to call me Kandi, Bae or Boo.
I boasted about the things I was going to do to him when we
finally made love.
Warning him, one night with me will forever change his life.
I anxiously prepared the perfect candles, lingerie, music and wine.
My confidence was at an all-time high as my nerves surprisingly
misbehaved.
I winked at myself in the mirror remembering the things he said he like
I was going to do this. I was going to mess him up when I did that.
I tensely exhaled through clenched teeth as I heard him turning my
door knob.
Calmly reminding myself… I don't just talk the talk; I walk the walk.
I exchanged pleasantries with him as I welcomed him into my sacred
world.
"Yes Girl. It's. About. To. Go. Down." are the words I nervously
repeated to myself.
I judged by his demeanor, he had no idea the incredible night in store
for him.
Executing my plan, I boldly closed the distance between us with a
hug and kiss.
I rocked and rolled to the rhythm of his funky beat once I caught his wa
Within minutes, things took an unexpected turn not previously calculate
by me.
I clutched his back hoping to steady the flow and slow down my beating
heart.
Begging my immaculate skills not to betray me as my body seemed
confused.
I noticed my eyes rolled in the back of my head with each passing secon
No worries… there might still be time to recover from this
roller coaster ride.

I witnessed my legs were shaking and my voice was trembling uncontrollably.
Screaming to my inner freak, please show up and show out right now.
I noticed this love-making contradicted how I bragged this night would go.
There may not be any coming back from this as I have lost total control.
I surrendered it all as he smiled and my soul left my body over and over again.
Exhausted from the journey, I told myself I would get him the next time Girl.
I murmured these dreadful words in his ear as I came down from my high.
Baby… What's my name? Did he call me Kandi, Bae or Boo?

That Space

I want to occupy that space...
That space where nobody is supposed to be.
That space sworn to vacancy after the last rendezvous with love.
That space reserved dearest to your heart but the toughest to reside.
That space where "us", "we", and "our" precede every word spoken.
That space only dreamed and wished after life's disappointments and bad choices.

I want to occupy that space...
That space less guarded and tip-toed around as we talk the night away.
That space holding your deepest secrets, fears, failures, let downs and disappointments.
That space protecting your unspoken dreams, goals, wants, desires and sacred love.
That space hoping someone will motivate and help cultivate the man you desire to remain.
That space only dreamed and wished after life's disappointments and bad choices.

I want to occupy that space...
That space seeping through your smile when I walk in a room.
That space I can taste every time our tongues do their familiar dance.
That space I can feel illuminating from your skin as I caress you ever so gently.
That space where your eyes tell me what your heart is not willing or ready to say.
That space only dreamed and wished after life's disappointments and bad choices.

I want to occupy that space...
That space you are more comfortable than any space in the universe.
That space we make beautiful music all night long and our song can be heard over and over again.

That space our unspoken words of admiration for each other speak louder than our awkward silence.
That space where loyalty, trust, honesty and respect are our only rules.
That space only dreamed and wished after life's disappointments and bad choices.

I want to occupy that space...
That space.... That space... That space....

LOVING HIM

Kissing

Passionately kissing
Your Soul
A thousand miles away

This Love

T*his Love* is unexplainable, but undeniable.
Simply put… you get me, I get you.
My bad days become your let's fix it days.
Your good days become my let's celebrate days.
Your eyes ignite something deep in my soul.
My presence ignites something behind your smile.
Unspeakable joy exchanges from my heart to your soul.
Trusting you is effortless, but unnatural.
Your loyalty to me is undeserving, but treasured.
We undeniably can't explain *This Love*.

This Love is uncomplicated, but challenging.
Your vibe entices my vibe causing total surrender to you.
My Gucci attracts your Gucci causing total submission to me.
Your protection gently shields my exposed vulnerability.
You beautifully love me in unimaginable ways.
Instinctively, my prayers cover you as they cover me.
Every day's adventures test us with every opportunity.
Battling through distance, time and availability is exhausting.
Somehow passion draws us closer wanting more.
We challengingly wouldn't complicate *This Love*.

Love Colored Vision

With satisfaction dripping from her lips
Last night was what her body needed.
She clumsily left his embrace and his bed.
Her legs seemed weak and under his spell.
The walk to her car seemed impossible.
Love colored vision confused her.

As he stood outside the car for one last kiss
She held it together long enough to say goodbye.
She inserted different keys into the car's ignition.
No longer knowing how to operate her vehicle
Fumbling to put the car in gear.
Love colored vision confused her.

Her senses didn't leave his bed with her
Suddenly, every "O" on the street signs looked like hearts.
Shaking her head as she realized she was tripping
Flashes of the last 24 hours replayed in her mind.
She had to stop herself from turning her car around.
Love colored vision confused her.

Chills ran up and down her spine at her desk.
Each passing hour seemed to get longer and longer.
All she wanted to do was go home and sleep.
Somehow, she found herself in the car
On her way to chase the thrill of the last 24 hours.
Love colored vision confused her.

Love Colored Vision~
Pt 2.

W ith contentment rested on his lips
Last night confirmed he couldn't live without her.
He reluctantly loosen her from his embrace.
His fingers fumbled the small, velvet box.
The charisma of this woman was breathtaking.
Love colored vision confused him.

As she stood on her tip-toes for one last kiss
He traced the outer lining of her gorgeous face.
He had to control himself as his mind began to wander.
No longer able to think of anything or anyone else
Feeling like he couldn't wait one more day to make her his.
Love colored vision confused him.

His thoughts were warped with visions of them.
Suddenly, he smelled her perfume lingering in the air.
Shaking his head because this woman had him tripping
Flashes of their love making replayed in his mind.
He had to stop himself from showing up at her job.
Love colored vision confused him.

Nerves got the better of him while holding the ring.
Each passing minute seemed to go by slower and slower.
All he wanted to do was come up with the perfect proposal.
Somehow, he fell on his knees without the extras

As she opened the door, the chase had come to an end.
Love colored vision confused him.

KATRINA A. McCAIN

LOVING OTHERS

My Unexpected Blessing

I hear you calling my name while I'm carrying on with my day.
I hear your sweet little giggles as I tickle your tiny toes.
I hear your heart as love sends chills down my spine.
I hear God's tranquility, peace and love surrounding you.

I smell your unique scent in my clothes over my perfume.
I smell adoration as I steal a thousand kisses from you.
I smell healing, prosperity and God's favor on you.
I smell the beautiful future God has laid out for you.

I see goosebumps on my arms when I reflect on our bond.
I see the way you lovingly look at me and fondly admire me.
I see you bringing out the very best in me every day.
I see a virtuous woman chasing after God's heart.

I taste your trusting imagination, as I teach you new things.
I taste every delightful moment we spend together.
I taste the purest love God has ever given me through you.
I taste victory in everything you do, say or touch.

I touch blissful emotions every moment I think of you.
I touch my heart because I'm so grateful God chose me for you.
I touch your soul while teaching you the ways of God.
I touch heaven's doors every time you call me NaNa.

The Day I Became Me

The happiest and lowest days deposited different character trai
One life-changing event after another made undesirable
choices for me.
Those defining moments overrode innocence and plans for my life.
Unmistakably contributing small amounts to the person I would
ultimately be.
Unquestionably, the day I became me always leads back to the
gift of you.

On the day I became me, your tiny hands taught me the warmest
compassion.
I promised to hold your hands through whatever life throws at you.
As your hands grew bigger than mine, my heart expanded as wide
as a river.
Cheering you on near and far can be heard like a thunderous applau
As I tattooed your name on my heart, my dedication to you knows
no bound.

On the day I became me, your pretty brown eyes educated me on
unconditional love.
Since the moment you entered this world, every day has uniquely
never been the same.
Your love overtook my senses and became my driving force behind
me becoming me.
My hopes and dreams quickly changed to you, your future,
your hopes and your dreams.
Promises of forever from me to you have never been forgotten,
not honored or unfulfilled.

Twenty-three years later, you still shape me into me as the world shapes you into you.
No doubt, each test or trial poured small amounts of me along the way. However, the defining moment to me becoming me was indisputably the gift of you.
No love motivated me, pushed me or inspired me more than you and your love.
Unquestionably, the day I became me always leads back to the gift of you.

My Plus One

S tanding at our altar of love
We vowed to always honor each other.
From the first precious moment, we really saw each oth
Life wouldn't be the same apart.
I couldn't ask God for a better person to experience this life.
You always held my hand and fought my battles.
Obstacle after obstacle your stance became more solid.
Never have your loyalty wavered or been questioned.
Things seem one sided between us; often times they are.
Today I had the strength to carry us
Tomorrow you are the stronger one.
Where I am weak, you are bold.
Where I am courageous, you are timid.
People constantly try to figure our relationship
Fights occur between us often.
In the midst of disagreements
Our relationship continues to strengthen.
We reflect on the vow promised to each other.
As God elevates you to the next level
I can count on your hand to reach down for me.
As God provides a window for me to shine
My shadow is always warmed by you.
Together we are greater than we are apart.
Some things are just felt blindly by the heart
As I humbly thank My Plus One.

"ABOVE ALL, LOVE EACH OTHER DEEPLY, BECAUSE LOVE COVERS OVER A MULTITUDE OF SINS."

John 15:12

HEARTBREAK

My Married Man

My deepest and darkest secret is
I am in love with My Married Man.
I let him in with the pretense of being a friend.
I quickly fell in love with everything about him
His charm, his love, his support and his work ethics.
During our courtship, he often dropped unwanted clues.
There was always a situation I needed to understand.
Everything he did was out of obligation and not love.
One day, I noticed others riding on our Express Train of Love.
The other passengers looked so differently than me.
The same expressions of love were on their faces.
Could anyone get a ticket on our Express Train of Love?
Tickets piled up on the shattered floor of my expectations.
Could My Married Man really be wed to another?
I didn't want to share My Married Man.
Not being invited to family events or celebrations
Red flags flew higher than my love for him.
Unanswered questions raged deeply between us.
It didn't matter because his heart and soul were mine.
I continued to pretend My Married Man loved only me.
My heart won the battle my mind was so willing to lose.
With less time spent on me and our conversations.
I assumed more time spent on them and their conversations.
No longer able to excuse another lie
My selfishness and dignity took over my senses.
I picked up my pride and brushed off my ego.
With tears streaming down my face, I ran as fast as I could
Through the unlocked back door of our Express Train of Love.
My non-refundable ticket blew away in the wind.
I know it's sad that my deepest and darkest secret is
I am still in love with My Married Man.

My Million Dollar Smile

I blind the room by my million-dollar smile.
My million-dollar smile can't fool everybody.
Can't fool anybody that really sees me.
Really seeing me is a deep and penetrating thing.
A deep and penetrating thing captures me slowly.
Capturing me slowly paralyzes all my senses.
Paralyzing all my senses becomes my new struggle.
My new struggle is trying to stay away from you.
Staying away from you seems cold and emotionless.
Cold and emotionless sends the wrong message.
The wrong message destroys our uncertain future.
Our uncertain future seems lost and without purpose.
Lost and without purpose unfortunately causes doubt.
Causing doubt brings about a lack of trust.
Lack of trust hardens both our guarded hearts.
Our guarded hearts cope by acting cold.
Acting cold brings unwanted misunderstandings.
Misunderstandings react selfishly and hurtfully.
Selfishness and hurtfulness should not be our love story.
Our love story should reflect our mutual attraction.
Our mutual attraction means nothing sometimes.
Nothing sometimes means everything unspoken.
Everything unspoken sounds louder than words.
Louder than words isn't heard by us anymore.
Us anymore continues to struggle to survive.
Struggling to survive and thrive for what purpose?
What purpose was never questioned before.
Questioned before was always understood.
Always understood is now misunderstood.
Now misunderstood hurts beyond words.
Beyond words still lies my feelings for you.
My feelings for you are stronger than steel.

Stronger than steel was our determination.
Our determination was to keep us alive.
Keeping us alive has been replaced with a different story.
A different story hopefully isn't the end of us.
The end of us will never damage our love for each other.
Our love for each other can never be destroyed.
Can never be destroyed by my million-dollar smile.

Failure

Not getting the ring wasn't failure
Failure was present from the very start.
Nights I stroked your beard
I sensed the tension in your brows.
Your eyes darted around the room
Avoiding the contact you once longed.
Your body jumped from my touch.
What was familiar was no longer desired.
Where did you leave you before you came home to me?
Not hiding well behind your unhealed heart
The brick wall let a small amount of love peak through.
Willing to love you through your pain
Somehow you missed the presence of my pain.
Love just isn't enough sometimes!
Your half-truths disappointed me.
My lack of interest disappointed you.
Nothing much became your constant rebuttal
Okkkk followed by silence became mine.
What happened with the fellows… nothing much… okkkk!
What's on your mind… nothing much… okkkk!
What did you do today… nothing much… okkkk!
I knew you had an appetite for other women.
I smelled the betrayal when your resistance was weak.
Not wanting to hear what I already knew
I avoided the subject just like you did.
Trust was no longer our friend.
I failed our dreams and goals too
As I found comfort in the arms of another.
I realized the ring would only seal our failure.
Standing before our future uttering lies…
"Til Death Do Us Part."

Resentment would be too hard to handle.
Surely it would show up to fight our relationship.
Karma has already taken its ugly toll.
Our safe haven has been destroyed like broken glass.
Not willing to fight an already lost battle
We rest uneasily in our comfortable bed of deception.
Lies, half-truths, pain and betrayal were our failure.
We reached failure long before thoughts of a ring.

Too Quiet

The world went quiet... too quiet
As I screamed my truths in my head.
I am angry! I am upset! I am pissed!
The more I do right by people
The shorter my end of the stick becomes.
When I think of the people who wronged me
They seem to be living their best lives.
Where is my best life?
Pictures paint scenarios that are not always true.
I was insecure moments before taking my last picture.
Several retakes showed different imperfections.
Torn between which angle would be liked the best.
I deleted all of them in my silence

The world went quiet... too quiet
The lack of support from people reminded me of my silence.
Friends used to be on all sides when I stretched my arms out.
Yes, life goes on. Yes, things change.
I would have never guessed some people would be those changes.
They and I were supposed to be forever.
Broken too much to talk to them, I move through each day pretending
Pretending to be the happiest person in the room.
My pain allows me those good hours in the presence of others.
It awaits me as soon as I sit in my silence.

The world went quiet... too quiet
When I encourage myself I am doing the right thing.
I have nothing else but God to rely on and he hasn't forgotten about
me.
Especially when another man means me no good in my silence.
Another bill lays in the mailbox breaking my silence.

Awaiting test results from CT Scans as the anxiety shatters my silence.
I have nothing else to rely on but God when the tears get too heavy
to hold.
God becomes my strength when the silence seems too loud.
The world went quiet… too quiet
When I put on the perfect song that usually consoles me.
The empty wine glass on the counter top doesn't bring any noise.
Reciting the perfect poem in my head seemed too quiet.
Thoughts of hooking up with someone intensifies the silence.
My silent screams break nothing but my loud thoughts.
Where do I find noise, as the world went quiet… too quiet?

Us Without You

I seem stable, controlled and put together so well
Until I speak your name.
Oh, how good your name tastes in my mouth!
As the dreadful, painful memories pound against reality
I lay in the bed of our pure bliss, fighting against the truth.
Before I start this day, my mind plays tricks on me.
Did you really touch my soul and leave me with broken pieces?
Those broken pieces of my heart no longer fit.
Or did I rearrange me to fit Us and my soul tied to Us
But yours not to Us, as you continue to move Without Us.
Once the greatest lovers of all times
Now strangers drifting through life without Us.
The sparkle in my eyes dimmed the day we closed the door on Us.
Did the sparkle in your smile dim by the mere thought of losing Us?
Each day I lose a little more of Us.
The wheels of my life continue to turn without Us.
Do they make you happy?
Or do you continue to draw from your strength within?
I promise you I gave you all of me
Even my hidden parts not exposed to others.
How could you be in the arms of others when my heart still longs for
Us?
My body feels betrayed at the thought of someone else caressing it.
I often hear and feel the things you did to me when you made
love to me.
When will you stop betraying my thoughts?
I'm trying to move on as you've moved on without Us.
I really miss you in ways I'm not sure you've been missed before.
I crave your uplifting motivation and selfless advice.
I miss being your support as you pretended to need Us.
I know I needed Us.
Do you miss me, my soothing voice, my infectious laugh?
My love, my support, my undying devotion and dedication?
I was only trying to fix your hurt not even caused by Us.

Not able to stop dreaming of you with my eyes wide open
My heart closes shut as it continues to heal without Us.
Nothing left to do but to release Us from my heart and my soul
Since this relationship was played out more in my mind than in reality.
Where will this love I try to deny go each morning I wake without Us?
Or will I wake up one day and Us will be a mere memory in my existence?
Until God reveals the whens, wheres and whys about Us
I will continue to do Us Without You!

BECAUSE SHE DECIDED TO LOVE

KATRINA A. MCCAIN

SOCIAL ISSUES

Beautiful Black Man

Saluting you, Beautiful Black Man, is such an honor to do.
I can't think of anyone who stands taller and firmer than you.
Even when the world diminishes you
Think you will never amount to anything
I see prestige and royalty, my Beautiful Black Man.
Your influences change communities, the nation, even the world.
Do you know how powerful you are?
God placed a secret drive deep in the walls of your heart.
The sky is the limit to the amazing things you can accomplish.
Your steadfastness is contagious as you move mountains.
Daily, you fight racism in an unjust and unrewarding society.
The world treats you unfairly my Beautiful Black Man.
Your secret prayer closet is where you fight your battles.
The world's cuts, bruises and insults don't faze you.
You turn them into motivation as your ambition soars even higher.
Your swag, my Beautiful Black Man, is so authentic
Never to be duplicated!
Commanding attention as you walk in the room is your best
impression.
Nothing is more attractive than your determination.
You see a vision when others see darkness.
You see a dream when others see nothing.
Your protection is more inviting than the sun on a winter's day.
Keep making positive moves my Beautiful Black Man.
Keep your head up when life throws its hardest punch.
Please know you are appreciated, loved, treasured and adored.
I see you, Beautiful Black Man!
I see your heart, Beautiful Black Man!
I see your soul, Beautiful Black Man!
Saluting you, Beautiful Black Man, is such an honor to do.

It's Cold In Here

I t's cold inside the walls of Family Court.
"Justice for All" is bigger than the sun
Plastered on the pale, white wall.
Somehow, its warmth isn't felt by all
Who occupy the hard, wooden seats.
Organized chaos is the unique design
Moving people along this dramatizing day.
People whisper in various conversations.
Some are praying for a victorious outcome
Others' only concern is the order of the docket.
Lawyers argue with each other
After having their morning coffee together.
Judges become numb to this emotionless setup
As they feel this coldness every day.
I'm confused how my hot, raw emotions
Are not breaking the coldness of this Justice System.
My love usually warms any environment
Except Family Court!
Kids waiting at home are clueless
The unfair battles fought inside these cold walls.
Parents throw boiling, hot insults at each other
As if winning this battle proves anything.
Immaturity and selfishness are center stage
But does nothing to break the thick ice.
The coldness of name calling and blaming
Is heard in every unfortunate case.
Hot, bitter words are thrown around dipped in pain
Proving coldness runs through everyone's veins.
Fire and devastating wrath are felt
From different angles in Family Court.
"Justice for All" attempts to shield every baby
From the coldness and fire

Exchanged inside the walls of Family Court.
Somehow, sitting on this hard, wooden seat
All I can say is… It's Cold in Here.

Sad State of Affairs

S ecrets and Lies
Running rampant on the doorstep
Exposed for the world to see.
The broken government
Of the greatest country
Worldwide it used to be.
Millions are to blame
Democracy exploited
Our rights to vote were key.
Destroyed from the inside
Without added protection
Ruled by dishonesty.
Underhanded deals
Made with sworn enemies
Rock our nation's security.
Fighting across party lines
Mission to only win
Abandoning all loyalty.
Separating children from families
With Border Protection
Corruption is our enemy.
Creed surpasses innocence
My child is watching
With eyes filled with glee.
Protecting and shielding
God help us please
Cries from bended knee.
Answers already provided

Seek his face and humble ourselves
God will heal our country.
(2 Chronicles 7:14 GW Translation)

Our Own Disparity

E arned rights from previous generations
Are getting choked by our own pride
In weakened communities.

Pain seared in another mother's heart
As she says goodbye too soon
To her son with untapped potential.

Unnamed bullets pierced the foundation
Of one family's safety net
As their daughter sleeps in her bed.

Controlled by bloody pledged alliances
Streets become the new playground
For Black on Black Crime.

Instant satisfaction replaces hard work
Causing our kids to seek fast money
While more dope is pushed in addictive arms.

Parents leave responsibilities created by them
As children fight unfairly in a world
Designed to bind them with chains.

Uninspired kids watch through tainted eyes
As generational curses sweep rapidly
Through our unprotected veins.

New religious beings challenge older saints
With less education and worldly knowledge

But can't testify to the goodness of Jesus.
Support from people who don't look like us
Can be counted on more than
The ones breaking bread from the same table.

Accepting that's the way it supposed to be
Dreams and goals stop inspiring us
And we sink deeper in our own disparity.

RELIGIOUS

Gently

Moon replaced by dawn
Soft wind kisses mountaintop
Ever so gently.

Sun chased away night
Crashing wave touches beaches
Ever so gently.

Stars exchanged darkness
Mild breeze caresses dessert
Ever so gently.

Nature offered bliss
Beauty provides by God's love
Ever so gently.

Amazing Love

Amazing
Amazing most
Amazing most is
Amazing most is God
Amazing most is God Love

Love God is most amazing
Love God is most
Love God is
Love God
Love

What God Knew That Day
(Genesis Chapter 2)

I can only imagine what God knew that day he made Man. *(Romans 11:36)*
God knew Man would fail him many times. *(Matthew 26:41)*
   Often longing for things Man is not supposed to have, *(Ecclesiastes 1:8)*
One apple would bring much corruption and greed. *(Genesis 2:16-17)*
God immediately put in place a Salvation Plan. *(John 3:16)*
God would send his son Jesus to save Man. *(2 Corinthians 5:18-20)*
Knowing Man was not worthy,
God promised Man eternity in spite of his sins. *(John 10:28-30)*
Creating Man was never an option though,
God loved Man so much. *(Romans 5:8)*
Desiring to mold an imperfect Man in human flesh,
God breathed his precious breath of life in Man. *(Genesis 2:7)*
I can only imagine God stepping back and admiring his handsome beauty.
Smiling at his perfect, imperfect masterpiece.
God cared about the desires of Man's heart. *(Psalm 20:4)*
Giving Man free reign throughout the land,
God put Man in charge of all the animals. *(Genesis 2:19-20)*
Because God still did not want Man lonely,
God immediately thought of the perfect helpmate for Man. *(Genesis 2:18)*.
Causing a deep sleep to fall upon Man,
God removed a rib from Man's body and created Woman. *(Genesis 2:21-23)*
How blessed am I, God found favor in me.
Long before I was formed in my Mother's womb? *(Galatians 1:15)*
Fast forwarding our lives and backing them up at the same time,
God knew he made two imperfect people to be perfect together.
God commanded Man to sprinkle this world with His love. *(John 13:34)*
Help our neighbors when they are in need. *(Matthew 25:35-36)*
Teach our kids and the younger generations Godly principles. *(Deuteronomy 6:6-9)*
Each generation of Man grows stronger and wiser.
Never to leave the foundation of who Jesus Christ is.
In this wicked world of today, when fortune and fame are more dominant;
I can only imagine God smiling at his perfect, imperfect creation.
Only God knows What God Knew that Day he made Man.

I Pray

I pray for you even when you are not in my presence.
I pray you see yourself as God so lovingly sees you.
I pray for your soul and God enters your heart like never before.
I pray God's faithful hands continue to cover your life.
I pray God heals your hidden pain and your broken places.
I pray for good health and a long life for you and your blood line.
I pray no attack from the enemy will ever succeed or prosper.
I pray everything you touch in this life will be blessed.
I pray God continues to order your steps like the righteous person you
I pray you are well and all of your needs and desires are met.
I pray you continue to strive for your hopes and dreams in your later ye
I pray for your happiness and protection over your hopes and dreams.
I pray you never settle or become complacent with this life.
I pray you never struggle financially, emotionally or spiritually again.
I pray God gives you the necessary wisdom for every situation in life.
I pray genuine love surrounds you every day of your life.
I pray for good support for you whether it's family or friends.
I pray your own expectations of people do not disappoint you or let
you down.
I pray for discernment for you to know who is good or not for your life.
I pray you feel valued, loved and respected every day of your life.
I pray you continue to be your unique self even when life deserves
differently.
I pray for forgiveness for you as you give it and receive it.
I pray you lack nothing as you provide for yourself and your family.
I pray you are the best parent and guidance your children need.
I pray God's protection over your life and your family's lives.
I pray you remain a strong, dependable pillar in your family.
I pray your family can always lean, depend and count on you.
I pray you know one day how you truly impacted my life.
I pray you know how sacred our bond is and I will always protect it.
I pray you know my love for you runs deeper than the perfect words.

I pray you know my heart still skips a beat every time we talk.
I pray you know there will never be another you and me in this lifetime.
I pray you know I'm so thankful our paths cross so many years ago.
I pray you see God had a purpose in us meeting one another.
I pray a Prayer of Thanksgiving because life has not torn us apart.
I pray our friendship strengthens as the years continue to roll.
I pray everyone experience this type of genuine, selfless love as we have.
I pray I love you and you love me as deeply as we do in this moment forever.

In My Love

Exhausted from another night with no sleep.
I wiped away the tears racing down my face.
This thing has had a hold on me for months now.
Trying to twist out of its grasp
My only desire is to get through another day.
The water mixed with my tears as I stand in the shower.
In the stillness of that moment
My doubts and fears controlled me.
I heard God saying to me this will not last always.
I've been struggling but I trusted God to see me through.
Eagerly waiting for him to comfort me.
I held my breath for a few moments.
Excitement burst through my soul
My Father began talking to me once more.
My dear beloved child, always remember I am here with you.
I am not blind to what you are going through right now.
Just hang on a little while longer.
This too shall pass My Love.
You are stronger than you think.
You have struggled before.
I have always brought light to your dark situations
Carried you through many storms unharmed and unscathed.
Please rely on me to get you through this thing too.
Keep your faith strong during these tough times.
Believe my promises and you will have victory.
You get some rest now My Child.
Take your hands off this thing.
I will handle this thing from now.
I know what you need to build your character.
You will be amazed at what's in store for you.
Dry your eyes and experience the fullness of my joy.
I love you more than you can ever imagine.

Sealing that precious moment with a kiss.
God left as quickly as he came.
All I could hear through the tears was
In My love, God.

KATRINA A. McCAIN

FINAL MESSAGE OF LOVE

My Love Story

W hat God Knew that Day" was a perfect love story
Would be birthed from the pages of creativity.
Humbly, I recited words in the midnight hour.
"That Space" was created through obedience.
"Love Colored Vision" slowly began to manifest on paper.
"The Day I Became Me" was hidden "Gently" in each line
As "My Blemished Past" became "Too Quiet".
"Butterflies and a Perfect Stranger in Dark Lights"
Describe different versions of "Who Am I".
"I Pray" my "Amazing Love" is revealed in each poem.

Poetry became "My Unexpected Blessing"
While creating an "Old Photo" of this journey.
After "Failure" and dealing with "Cancer Never Takes a Vacation",
"One Dance" with God utterly altered my "Sad State of Affairs".
"Million Dollar Smile" and "Kissing" displayed my gratitude.
"This Love" experienced with God is mind blowing.
There is nothing better than God and "Pancakes in the Morning"
"Before Momma Came Home."

When times were tough and my dream seemed so far away
Even in "Our Own Disparity" and "It's Cold in Here"
God often asked me, "What's My Name?"
No longer wanting to do "Us Without You"
God constantly became "My Plus One" "In my Love".

If "Because She Decided to Love"
Is sincerely felt by one *Beautiful Black Man*
I have accomplished what I set out to do
With the completion of this project.
No more "Harmless Lies" and constant "Bleep, Bleep" fighting.
Please always remember "My Married Man"
"Anything Doesn't Go with a Scorpio".

THANK YOU FOR YOUR SUPPORT

FOLLOW POET KATRINA:
FACEBOOK & INSTAGRAM
@POETKATRINAMCCAIN

Made in the USA
Columbia, SC
30 October 2019